Earthsongs

50 Poems

50 Sketches

Robert Eugene Perry
poet

Ferol Anne Smith
artist

D1403321

Published by Human Error Publishing
www.humanerrorpublishing.com
paul@humanerrorpublishing.com

ISBN: 978-1-948521-78-9

Cover design
by
Paul Richmond
and
Robert Eugene Perry

Poet Statement:

This collaboration with my artist friend Ferol was absolutely a labor of love. In discussing the sketches that would accompany the poems, she intuitively grasped the meaning of the words and translated them into sublime images. She needed very little direction from me.

It was almost as if the synchronicity of the project was palpable to both of us. Her sketches added a new dimension to my own perception of my poems. This has been one of the most rewarding artistic experiences of my life.

Artist Statement:

When Bob first approached me about this project, I was intrigued. Normally, my art requires creatively rendering a visual scene. For this project, it would involve interpreting the written word.

At first, it was a challenge to read a poem and conceptualize a complementary nature scene. However, once I started to really grasp the essence of his words, the process became much easier. His poems inspired me to reach within, and as a result I gained a deeper appreciation and understanding of his work.

Acknowledgements

Conjunction (Perryville Dam)
Pierpont Meadow
Susurration

Published in
Honoring Nature Anthology, 2021

*

The Invitation
Self-Pity Speaks
Gratitude Answers
Transcendence

Originally published in the novel
Where The Journey Takes You
Robert Eugene Perry, 2007

*

Wormtown to Woo
Galleria Mall Rats
Turning Point (Elm Park)
The Inn at the Square

Published in
Worcester Magazine 2021

Published by Human Error Publishing
www.humanerrorpublishing.com
paul@humanerrorpublishing.com

Dedication

Poet:

A debt of gratitude for all those who have accompanied me along this winding path – most especially Krissy, Joshua, and Zachary who make life an adventure. For my parents Bob & Carol who left this world too soon, and who left their mark on me. And for you who have come to read this book, may you find inspiration, solace and challenge in its pages.

Artist:

To my husband Ethan, for your never ending support, guidance and insight. Thank you for being on this journey with me, you are a power of example. To my friends and family who continually encourage and motivate me, I am truly grateful for all of you.

Earthsongs

WATER

EARTH

AIR

WATER

Conjunction (Perryville Dam)

This is the sweet spot
where time slows.

The marsh explodes with sound:
red wings caw
full throated joy
calling to make life –

a wood drake observes
from the channel
patiently awaiting
his chance to impress.

Slowly moving water
heading for cataracts
                just downriver.

Patchwork of greens and browns
new growth sprouts from decay.

The river flowing over the dam
background music for the bog
bright red buds on trees
highlighted by overcast skies.

Standing on the bones of my ancestors
I am here, now.

Everything Belongs

I am a tree, grown up
twisted and gnarled from
bending backwards towards
the light, having spent
too much time
in shadow.

I am a stream, flowing
hither and yon, picking up
stuff meandering through
strange lands, sometimes singing
often murmuring seeking
an ocean.

I am a cloud, pursuing the heights
blown about and set off course
filled with moisture and vapors
stretched out and dissipated
at times reflecting the colors
of the sun.

I am the Universe, born of stardust
a miracle of contradictions
energy and matter, moving and static
constantly changing and adapting
neither created nor destroyed, only
Being.

Many Rivers

Time turns through the seasons
    under canopies of golden trees
        change, the only constant
            like the undulating of the seas.

            I have searched for all the answers
        to find the ties that bind
    one god in many variations
uniting humankind.

Denying my naïveté
    I set sail for the grail
        looking for the blessed chalice
            convinced I could not fail.

            What a rude awakening
        to crash upon the shore
    of my own illusions
and at my own backdoor.

When we saw others solve their problems by a simple reliance upon the Spirit of the Universe...

I have always felt compelled to read
book after book, fiction, non
fiction, sacred texts, commentaries, treatises
poetry, myth, fables, always seeking for answers
to the big questions.

Doctrine, dogma, diatribes
religion, rites, ritualization
contemplation, over
intellectualization – all complicate
the basic situation.

How many years now have I asked
why am I here now, tried
to swallow the fear now, traded
this for that idea now. Could it really
be this clear now?

A simple reliance
upon the Spirit of the universe
breathing in, breathing out
letting
     go.

Piermont Meadow

Bare feet on the grassy path
Spring births unparalleled joy
This conduit between worlds
Grass gives way to rough needles

Tall pines arch
A portal to silence, introspection
Whispers weaving through the forest
Evergreen slicing my dull senses awake

A stream bends through
Marsh grass and cattails
Sliding under the path
To the waiting pond

Now the trail forks, to the right
A wooded path will reach the water
To the left will loop
Past the sunning beaver's dam

Cycles, seasons, changes –

The gestation of spring,
Dance of summer rhythms,
Circles of fall, all lie down
And sleep in winter.

Portals (*Douglas State Forest*)

So many paths
each trail a new exploration
subtle, you need to pay attention
to the portals between the trees
where moss gathers
another world awaits.

Your senses keen
dream awake another realm where
humans hunt, deer surrender
granting them another November,
balanced lives
and grateful hearts.

Sit beside the stream which
slips through the forest floor, more
than it seems carrying detritus nourishing
flora and fauna, over and under rocks
singing, splashing, gurgling, laughing
bringing life.

Woodpecker's rhythmic thrumming
signals change, impermanence –
new growth sprouts from dead rot
small creatures shelter in old stone walls
lichen covered bones of
yesterday's civilization.

When my mother left this world
I spent a week in mourning, the
arboreal inhabitants heard my cries
passed no judgement, and at last
her sigh on the evening
breeze.

All things ephemeral, memory migrates
from then to now, and back again
stories we tell weave the tapestry
connecting families, clans, peoples
dreaming a vision, forging a future.

Riverside Park in Autumn

Heron poised to strike his supper
sunlight plays upon the ripples
subtle questions come to mind:
where does this river begin?

Imagination paints a picture
snow melting on a mountain
runoff joining other streams
wending its way southwards

Waxing, waning, speeding, slowing
spending itself in joyful abandon
crossing imaginary boundaries
it makes its way to here, then

Flowing downwards, rolling
over fallen trees, swirling
into eddies by the bank, slowing
at the bend by the gazebo.

Lazy ducks float by, gazing
skyward at the geese flapping overhead
skies are clouding, wind
whispers of a change to come.

Snapshots from a Nemophilist

Haunter of woods, world
weary traveler, return to
mother loving earth dancer in
symbiotic sacredness.

Chickadees in choir, chirrup
dancing in the round, descending
surreal space between moments
only one remains, observing.

Winter on the cusp of spring,
gray day left a blue feather
sparkling like a jewel in the leaf clutter
unmoved by March winds.

Autumn into winter, crisping
golden eagle sudden rising
wingspan wider than the path
mouth agape in wide wonder.

red fox, red tail, red headed
pileated woodpecker, beaver
porcupine, snake, deer – all
tales to tell, omens to interpret.

Susurration

(in) a language all its own, the river
speaks in susurrus, syllables
sometimes sibilant, soft
slaps of waves over stones,
sweeping sensuously across branches,
swirling into eddies around corners,
speaking in soothing textures,
showing off its splendor –
singing surreptitiously
      for those with ears to hear.

Yugen

noun (Japanese)
A profound awareness of the universe
that triggers feelings too deep and mysterious for words.

echoes of the sea
calling
time out of mind
sunshine
laughter mixed with
salty tears.

EARTH

Unexpected Connections

You and I, my friend, we are
Inexorably intertwined.
Whither thou goest I have
Been, here or in a dream – sliding into
The collective unconscious – so many
Little synchronicities, all my
Idiosyncrasies mirror yours
Distinctively.

Albeit tacit, we are
All connected, taking this ride for
Such a short time – either getting busy
Living, or incrementally dying – moments slip
By in a trance, forgetting to dance, locked
Into routine, pulled by the slipstream of
Time falling behind, falling
In line.

Nature whispers her secrets in
Systemically recurring patterns
Healing refrains, soft echoes, rolling cadence;
Shouts in thunderous exclamations, fiery
Proclamations, howling winds and earth torn asunder
Hoping to wake us, to shake us, to make us
Connect with the larger Life before we
Go under.

26 seconds

Earthbeat pulses
Lost in wonder
Feet soil dancing
Wind as partner
Soaring skyward
Hawk as brother
Rapid descent
Catch the river
Otter rising
Making ripples
Calling brook trout
To the table
Grateful offering
We are oneing
All within this
Twenty six seconds.

From a writing meditation prompt by Kristen Leigh
5/15/21, regarding how the earth pulsates every 26 seconds.
The phenomenon has a quantitative measurement but a
mysterious origin.

axis mundi

between
heaven
and
earth

i
stand
a
conduit.

all
control

is
an
illusion.

Constant Companion

Who knew? God loves me
Whether I like it or
Not.

Looking from inside out, grace
Surrounds me, I breathe
Divinity.

I am not alone, never
Abandoned, always
Loved.

Struck dumb by that
Inescapable
Fact:

Where all I see is lack,
The truth is,

God
Has
My
Back.

Flatlining

How egregiously we sleepwalk our days
oblivious to the larger Life, reacting
not responding, waiting to speak
and not listening, missing life's
abundant opportunities.

Eschewing intimacy we settle for less by
buying more, hiding behind screens dumbing
down our dreams , embracing the
nonsensical, acting reprehensible
idolizing idiocy.

Alienated from ourselves and one another we
kill the planet again and again, choosing
convenience over conscience, choking off the
umbilicus of our Mother as we reap
our due reward.

It is not too late to discover our disconnect,
opening ourselves to a vision of the universal
awakening to each infinitesimal choice
softening our edges, stepping back from the ledges
becoming one Creation.

Fox Talks

She first showed up at twilight
A kit with her brother stealing glances
Among the stones outside her den.

Our mutual fascination was magic
I returned every night for weeks –
But foxes grow up fast.

Years later my dad passed away
I was alone in my truck at noontime
And fox walked right down the middle

Of the abandoned street. She came
Right up to my door and I asked her why
She was out in the middle of the day.

She winked at me and trotted off
Into the pine scrubs, leaving me
A memory larger than life.

Since then she has taught me invisibility –
How to walk through the forest
Without disturbing its inhabitants

And she has taught me how to stay silent
When I would speak and disturb
The perfection of the moment.

Galleria Mall Rats

We were all mall rats
wandering the galleria maze
looking for meaning, searching
for acceptance,

Grabbing scraps of love
from anyone, anything that
might make us feel we
belonged somewhere.

DiRado documented the scene
in black and white, mohawks and
misfits, spiked hair and
savoir faire for the 80's.

The mall died years ago, many
of its denizens did as well, those
of us who remain remember our
fallen by loving our lives today.

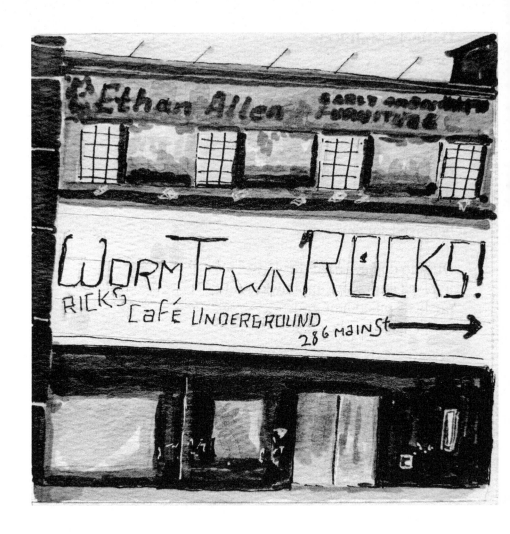

Wormtown to Woo

That 70's DJ named it Wormtown, just
trying to ignite the punk rock scene –
but every city has a seedy underbelly, so
the politicians and the admen objected, yet

Watch now!
Worms push through the offal, offering
fecundity to the soil, bringing
new life to arid landscapes.

A decade later I moved to the city,
greeted by the "Wormtown Rocks" scrawl
next to Rick's Café Underground, another
place those wonderful worms were at work.

Underground artists, musicians, poets
rise and fall, decades pass they
leave their mark or not, no city
is to blame for ignominy or fame – Now

we stole "The Woo" from England our
sister city, hoping to woo the bankers,
pumping up the urban renewal, white
washing our graffitied past –

Leaving a hollow sound where once
there was a roar.

inside out

the feeling begins, dark and cold:
      wanting – to black out the past
      hoping – to wait out the future
      longing – to shut out the present;

anger alongside apathy
      a toxic cocktail –
marinating in the mixture
      all seems hopeless, all seems

lost. that which is has been
a thousand times before.
i cannot smile, i cannot move to
rouse myself from this
deep lethargy.

sunlight ceases; trees appear as
cardboard cutouts, birdsongs become
noxious noise.

can death be other than this?

no comfort, no light, no whisper
of the spirit in this
dry land.

hold. hold now. hold on until...

receding to the shadows
the dark beast leaves its cold trail
and air begins to move again

...tomorrow dawns, bright and clear.

all my questions gone, fear
disappeared, panic managed, and
i am left wondering:

could it all be just a matter of perception?

the world is the same, but the view has changed
a shift occurred somewhere within
perhaps the pieces were rearranged
and God sits back with a knowing grin.

September in the Meadow

(Among the) golden rod and milkweed pods
late season bees still interlace
their mystical pollination patterns

A soft wind whispers through the field
weaving a blanket of quietude
sky and earth, spirit and environment

Deep connection, altered perception
awakening a longing for something
I cannot begin to name

The only sound heard
is the language of birds
fleeting and musical

This sanctuary breeds community
hemlock, pines, birch and beech
share the forest and the trails

Here in this moment lie all moments
thrumming in blissful harmony
everything exactly as it should be.

AIR

A Whisper Stilled

Ah –
who am I to disturb the universe
with my plights and gripes?

Indeed
where was I when the foundations
of the earth were laid?

I speak
without knowledge or understanding, yet,
I experience something like speech:

A whisper –
borne upon the wind when silence descends
and the mind is stilled.

still life

fruit bowl, oil on canvas a
still life of someone's table.
generations later it is life
captured in that moment.

still, life goes on when
the world is frozen
in a death like grip, still –
life will find a way.

life still has a way
of emerging from death, where breath
is stilled and life is slowed, till all
remains perfectly still.

after the vaccine slays the virus
and we have buried our own slain
only one question remains:
will we still take life for granted?

The Holy Fool

Crazy wisdom, crazy love
Begging bowl in hand
Dancing for the wind above
Singing for the sand

All is one and one is all
The motley saint exclaims
Heeding only ardor's call
Free from worldly chains

Making love to all the world
Pregnant with desire
Swimming in the sea of stars
Bathing in their fire

Calling all to join the dance
Partake of the divine
Leaving life's illusions here
And stepping out of time.

Truth Tellers

The night calls us together.

We enter the circle
drums hammering out
the rhythm of our hearts
a sacred unity, woven together
under the stars, or in the garage
the fire bears witness
to our fidelity.

Amidst the incense
we enter the silence.

Each soul naked before Creator
we turn our backs to the clock
and look within to find our truest selves.

Brought back by the bell
we sit in sanctified silence,
awaiting the spoken word.

We are truth tellers, all
the stories we tell about ourselves
weave the fabric of the universe.

Down (acrostic poem)

Down –
it always brings me
down.

yesterday,
only a memory
unless –

something changes.
everything fades...
everything.

the truth is,
however you view it,
everything changes.

we
always
yearn, yet

time will not stop.
here is where
eternity meets

polarity, the intersection
of the
endless with the
moment.

miraculous!
of all the
verities of
existence, time
stops for no one.
?

Faithfulness

Deep calls to deep
From the core of my soul
To yours.

We dwell so close
Yet still have space,
Intimacy
Creates this place

Where life is full
And family thrives,
The joy is real
And faith survives

The test of time
The twists of change,
We stay unique
But still the same:

Two in one flesh
Infused divine
Passion's purpose
Simply sublime.

Just beneath the waves
I feel myself sinking
into

      your

           embrace.

Finding and Abiding

When you are lost
I will show you the way Home.

Within yourself is where
I choose to dwell.

Yes, the kingdom of God
Is within you.

A whispered Word
Enwraps your soul –

Mystery unveiled
For those who wait.

Effortless

I watched the hawk soar this morning
Effortless, circular, graceful –
He flew under the upside down half moon
Which lay pale in the blue sky –

Primordial perfection.

Freedom in Humility

To turn the other cheek
As I have done before,
Proclaiming that I'm meek –
Not laying on the floor.

The world will try to force
Its way into my soul,
Clinging to the source
Steadfastness is my goal.

Humility a word
Society abhors,
Soars just like a bird
Above egoic wars.

Joyous is the one
To whom oneself is true,
Once devoid of avarice
The world belongs to you.

Learning to Surrender

Passions come and go
the quintessential undertow...

...and I am left
with nothing more
than just a rough idea
of what it is I should expect from this

and so I lay
my burden down, lay
my burden down, down

at the altar of forgiveness
into the Hands of healing

I lay my burden down, down
into the Arms of Love

all my sorrow,
all my pain,
all my hope,
all my longing

surrender.

FIRE

A Bad Seed

When I start
to feel good
what is in me
that says I shouldn't,
looks for a reason to supplant
that good feeling
with a bad memory?

Not good enough.

Who first uttered those words
planting that bad seed
in my youthful heart?

Through the years it has grown,
engulfing whole areas of my garden
as invasive and unwelcome as kudzu.

Not good enough.
Never
good enough.

What a
crock.

Bitter Bondage

What ails me thus is hard to speak
and so I wish to let it be,
not to turn and spill the beans
reveal my weakness and dark dreams.

Disgust will harden into shame
and I, the only one to blame
and what indeed can I explain? It draws me
       again and again.

And so I pray and try to leave
it in Creator's hands, yet still
the reservation's up my sleeve
and all my good intentions will
not stop the cycle, and it seems
the harder I try to look away
the more it will invade my dreams
and try to have its wicked way.

Clipse

There are no words to convey
the emptiness of the moment
when the light left your eyes.

We stood silent, speechless
in the wake of your passing.

There was no comfort in knowing
that you had passed beyond the pain
or that we made the right decision.

There was no comfort.

The hollow heaviness pressed down
squeezing out light and joy
leaving only the cold chokedamp
of loss.

Bodhicitta

(attaining great compassion for all sentient beings,
accompanied by a falling away of the ego)

1. Suffering

shards of glass, blue red lights road
slick with rain, viscous river of fluids
wailing sirens; other wailing, others waiting
staring deep not seeing not feeling gurneys
odd angles holding fractured forms shouting
rushing figures smoke inhaling crying out
help is coming just hold on gasping
overwhelming fumes vision
blurring, drift to
void –

2. Tonglen

hovering
ghost or angel
soaking up your pain
bleeding out compassion
remaining present, keeping intention
holding on and letting go
simultaneous heartbeat
separation is the

illusion

3. Impermanence

rubbernecking tourists
grumbling at the logjam, making
the sign of the cross as they pass –
sacred and profane are abstractions
to the dead and dying –
which in fact
every
body
is.

Power of Example
- for MC

All of us
    from time to time
        have wondered why

Pain and sorrow
    enter into
        our humble lives

And there are
    no easy answers
        to fit these questions

Life happens, we
    have the choice
        to respond or react

To give or
    take back, to rejoice or
        complain

To shut down
    or embrace
        the pain

The only way out is through
    and you have brought all of us
        with you

Ah, how beautifully
    you have enriched
        our simple lives!

Sojourner

Seeker of the truth, forlorn
　　　how often does the door seem barred
When logic leads with leaden form
　　　the heart and spirit become hard
And all the world seems cold and grey
　　　hopes and aspirations charred.

Embittered by lost sentiment
　　　ideals of youth become as chaff
You wonder where the hours went
　　　now that your life is cut in half
Indeed what is there left to say
　　　when death parades the final laugh?

Time's illusion weaves a shroud
　　　we slumber in its warm embrace
To question comfort – disallowed!
　　　when everything is in its place
Till Thanatos comes and rends the veil
　　　and we're left floating off in space.

Waking up is optional
　　　some prefer to somnambulate
Like zombies, walking dead through life
　　　leaving love and chance to fate
I will choose to choose each choice
　　　this legacy of love to create.

The Wound Exposed

Cold. Hard. Heavy. Lifeless.

Trusting the process I descend,
Laying down body and defenses
Breathing in life,
Breathing out life.

The ground is frozen, dark
Nearly devoid of life – but
Not quite.

Mother earth tends to the
Cold, dead place in Swadisthana –
Kneading the soil, stirring the
Wasteland to life.

Father sky breathes life into me
Slowly – catching here and
There rhythm falters –
Until the place of pain is revealed.

The breaking point is breached
A howl is heard from that silent place:
Air rushes in bringing life to the still
Deadness.

Out of the open wound
A song emerges – given before
My birth – lost, so many
Years ago. And yet:

Nothing is ever truly lost.
The song brings the healing,
Cauterizing the wound with
Sacred fire.

The scar remains, a symbol
Of my power
And the solemn call
To give it all away

I am love. I am lover. I am loved. I am whole.

Transcendence

Transcendence is that which we seek
When what we are is not enough
Adherence to our Maker's heart
Will keep us strong when seas get rough.

The water takes the downward path
Abandoning itself complete
Hear it bubble! Hear it laugh!
What joy! Surrender sounds so sweet.

Over hill and through the country
Bending, winding, twisting round
Acquiescing to its calling
To always seek the lowest ground.

Lose yourself within the current
The living waters wash anew
Dare to be more than you hoped for
And you will see those hopes come true.

Turning Point (Elm Park)

City life, winter – disconnected, disenchanted
feeling the walls close in; leaving the
three decker behind, trudging through urban
slush seeking substantiating solace.

Winding down narrow streets, avoiding ice
and too close cars, turning the corner:
a vision – a park with people laughing and
skating like in a Rockwell painting.

Spring comes, sound of children at play
old man with a fishing pole next to the iron bridge
lovers walk the path and laugh at the future
bees and blooms abound.

Summer Art in the Park, a joyous cacophony
blending seamlessly with jazz music; painted door
standing ajar near a tree beckons, a portal to
before, behind or beyond.

Autumn, foliage fills my senses
a heron waits by the water –
I give up all resistance, and
call Worcester my home.

Why I Must Go

I have waited
hoped for clarity
sought discernment
ignored disparity
prayed for wisdom
slaved for ego
directed gently
forced the issue.

Acceptance is
the only answer
resentment kills
like a cancer
sneaking in
a foe unseen
to steal your life
devour your dreams.

The answer lies in letting go
of all the things I think I know
and all the plans I thought were real
are only walls of hardened steel
which bind me to my expectations
poisoning my love relations
forcing me back in my head
where things are abstract,
cold, and
dead.

Freedom now from bitter chains,
        my own prison of demands –
the Master sings his sweet refrain,
        and frees the door with his own hands.

SKY/HEAVEN

Careful Not to Disturb
(the Delicate Ecosystem of My Dream)

Speaking presence in the moonlight
Ocean whispers through the foam
Calling to my rented room.
I leave my sleeping spouse
Wander to the shoreline
Hear the mermaids
Singing each to each
Walk upon the waves
Following the silver pathway
Of what might have been
Each heart's transmigration
Another posited parallel lifetime.

A quarter of a century together
Never seemed a probability
Children now grown
Pathways of their own.
Here in this twilight time
I stand at the nexus of all
Those possible permutations.
Casting off any vestige of regret
The stars recede in the ebony heavens
Looking directly into the heart of the sunrise
Your eyes reflect back all that I had ever longed for
And I wake, finding our hands entwined under the sheets.

Eternal Now

I cannot grasp eternity
    is throbbing right inside of me

How infinite and unseen God
    should so indwell this humble clod

Blown and tossed by passion's storms
    to past or future either borne

As one day flows into the next
    with all these petty things I'm vexed

Freely floating in time's wake
    I miss the chance to remonstrate

Against the forms which bind me fast
    this shadow world which cannot last

The bigger picture passed unseen
    I lapse into a waking dream

Where I renew my prayer again
    to be here now where I begin.

Fragility

so many things cannot be mended
    careless words cut to the quick
        leaving a wound like an ice pick
        hard to see, yet running deep
    coloring our wake and sleep
leaving so many lives upended

Self-Pity Speaks

O the suffering you have borne
Unjust rejection, neglect and scorn
The weight of the world that you have worn
Upon your weary shoulders

How you've earned a little rest
Tried and tired, oft hard pressed
No one knows just how depressed
You feel as you get older.

Come with me, and take your ease
Drink my tonic, you who grieve
I am someone who believes
In the victim they have made you

Lay your head now in my arms
I will keep you safe and warm
Shelter you from things that harm
And I will make you –

The envy of all that hate you.

Gratitude Answers

Through dark of night the Good will shine
And lead me towards the choicest vines
The decision mine, my will to yield
To the higher ground or the potter's field

I will rejoice, though all seems lost
Give my all, not count the cost
No sacrifice can be called too grand
To choose the Good, to make a stand

O selfishness, my soul's foul bane
Depart from me, ne'er be seen again!

October Ghosts

In October my ghosts don't wait for Hallows Eve
They come early to check out this year's foliage
To talk of times that were, reinterpreting memories
As we walk through the forest, each moment
A grace I could not see while they were alive
They tell me nothing is ever wasted, ever lost
Pay attention to the way things come back to you
Spend yourself extravagantly, like these trees
Let everything go and you will discover
You have had everything you needed all along.

Orphan

sitting at the ocean
feeling like an orphan
emptiness engulfing
swallowed in the mourning

sunlight anathematic
clouds bring welcome cover
gulls join in the keening, a
symphonic minor number

heaviness descending
tide is rising higher
desire to surrender
swallow all this water

lay there at the bottom
blissfully forgetting
returning to the Mother
the Ocean's never ending.

The Inn at the Square

The weeping prophet, Jeremiah
Lent his name to a city shelter
A bastion of safety from the cosmic wars
Addiction, homelessness, mental illness.

I washed back up there in the early 90s
Just a tie dye shirt and cutoff jeans
No home no family no friends no hope
Blaming it all on bad luck.

Broken for the last time, eyes opened
Kindness rendered, I surrendered
Compassion ripped off the pall of denial
Exposed and desperate I asked for help –

I was taught service, give it away
Become that which you learn to love
The life I wanted was there all along
Becoming human, all things are possible.

The Invitation

How would you address
A somnambulist?
Would you lead him awake
With a fairy's kiss?
Would you dance in the dark
For his dreams to see?
Would he know who I am
When he looked at me?

Come and find the truth
Drop your past behind
All you need is hope
And an open mind
Let your spirit soar
Leave your fear below
Faith will fill the cracks
In your shattered soul.

Let the journey start
Let the trumpets sound!
Every step you take
Is on hallowed ground
Every breath you breathe
Is the spirit's call
So will win the prize
Who surrenders all!

We Are All God's Poems

What separates me from you –

Only a thought, a construct the
Mind's way of sorting things out
Categorizing according to usefulness
Each entity in its path, desperately
Trying to validate its existence when
Truth is incontrovertible, separation
Unnatural. When I breathe the trees
Agree the sky expands and all
That divides creation falls away
Into the illusion it actually is and
We are all one – the two-legged, four-
Legged, winged and finned, each serving
A divine purpose that cannot be fulfilled
Without one another.

Robert Eugene Perry is a native of Massachusetts. After much travelling and soul searching he returned to his home state and discovered what it means to bloom where you are planted.

His first novel *Where the Journey Takes You*, a spiritual allegory combining poetry and prose, was published in 2007. This was followed by three collections of poetry *The Sacred Dance: Poetry to Nourish the Spirit* in 2008, *If Only I Were a Mystic, This Would All Come So Easy* in 2011, and *Surrendering to the Path* released by Human Error Publishing in 2020.

Perry hosted a poetry group for disabled individuals at the former New England Dream Center in Worcester MA, and has emceed the monthly Open Mic at Booklovers' Gourmet in Webster MA since May 2017.

Three poems were included in NatureCulture/ Human Error Publishing 2021 anthology *Honoring Nature*. Two of Perry's poems were published in Poetica Magazine's 2020 Mizmor anthology. He has had several poems published in Worcester Magazine, and his short story *In The Company of Trees* was published by WordPeace journal in 2021..

A metaphysical poet, he draws inspiration from spending time in nature, endeavoring to reveal connections between our higher selves and the natural world. He is a devoted husband and father of two grown boys.

Ferol Anne Smith lives and works in central New England. She creates art that focuses on local flora, fauna, and landscapes. Many of her paintings recreate scenes while on location.

Ferol studied at the Worcester Art Museum and New England School of Fine Art. She also completed a plein air workshop in Tuscany, Italy.

Many of her paintings have been exhibited throughout the area including Booklovers Gourmet in Webster, First Unitarian Church in Worcester, the Richard Sugden Library in Spencer and the Jacob Edwards Library in Southbridge MA.

She was featured in the "Sturbridge Villager" and more recently, one of her plein air paintings appeared on the cover of the "Uxbridge Times".

She paints on location and from her studio located in the historic Manchaug Mills building in Sutton, Massachusetts.

Ferol also enjoys hiking, kayaking and gardening with her husband.

Reviews

From works that weave and entice us full circle back to where we began, to the secrets of life best heard within the realms of silence, to the undeniable need for all species to lean, stand and uphold one another and finally arriving at portals that resonate of home – Robert gives us poetry that makes its own music and then dances flawlessly to the score. And we, eavesdroppers of his talent are left unable to choose a favorite even as we taste his words again and again.

Linda Jones McCarthy singer, songwriter and poet

Robert Eugene Perry has an incredibly wide and diverse palette that he works with in creating the beautiful poetry he writes. His poetry embraces nature and our place within the sacred web of life. His themes are complex and searching as with grieving and loss, Buddhist thought, nature, the elements, environment, and contemplating married life. This book of poems is meant to be picked up time and again, to steep oneself in, and to celebrate the gift of life we are born into.

Jason Grundstrom-Whitney author of *Bear, Coyote, Raven released* by Resolute Bear Press (Pushcart nominee 2020)

Earthsongs is a soulful combination of word and image that enhances the experience of contemplating our place in the universe. Perry and Smith engage us in an eloquent duet, singing our connection to the natural and spiritual realms.

Debra Horan, owner Booklovers' Gourmet, Webster MA

Earthsongs is a profound book of poems and illustrations electrified by a beloved collaborative discourse between poet Robert Eugene Perry and artist Ferol Anne Smith. It is comprised of 50 poems and 50 sketches that disseminate from five themes: Water, Earth, Air, Fire and Sky/Heaven. Do not be "fooled" by the title, this is a collection of poems that are a series of revelations, repentance and regrets. Most of all it is a sequence of poems linked together by a message of reconciliation; all things in the end come to pass and acceptance of love is all that matters. This is not a book to be taken lightly, it is one to humble and inspire.

Stephen DiRado, Art Professor in the Visual and Performing Arts, Clark University, Guggenheim Fellow.

Earthsongs is a wonderful collaboration between poet Robert Eugene Perry and artist Ferol Smith. The combination of images conjured by Perry's evocative words, entwined with the stark black and white pen and ink drawings--Perry's images made flesh of sorts--is inspired. The contents invite readers to ponder, linger, and slowly take in the love and care with which it has been created. Do not rush. Spending time with this book is a gift for tired, troubled, or weary souls, and those who simply thrill to encounter beauty.

Marjorie Turner Hollman, Author of the *Easy Walks* book series

Robert Eugene Perry takes you on a spiritual journey through his musings. You can feel the darkness in the world, but he offers you paths to serenity and joy. Daily, I read one of his poems for my own well-being!

Joe Fusco Jr, Worcester humorist/poet

Heartfelt, with insides out and outsides in, Earthsongs, in meditative poetry and with gorgeous illustration, is an environmental prayer. This book is a field guide, a meditation on navigating the human condition, the spirit and the wild. A disciple of the woods, Perry invites you along and it's an invitation you don't want to miss.

Candace R. Curran, author of *Playing in Wrecks*

Made in the USA
Middletown, DE
29 March 2022

63264614R00070